Step-by-Step
PROBLEM SOLVING

Grade 4

DISCARD

Frank Schaffer
An imprint of Carson-Dellosa Publishing LLC
Greensboro, North Carolina

Credits

Content Editors: Christine Schwab and Heather Stephan
Copy Editor: Barrie Hoople
Layout and Cover Design: Lori Jackson

 This book has been correlated to state, common core state, national, and Canadian provincial standards. Visit *www.carsondellosa.com* to search for and view its correlations to your standards.

Copyright © 2012, SAP Group Pte Ltd

Frank Schaffer
An imprint of Carson-Dellosa Publishing LLC
PO Box 35665
Greensboro, NC 27425 USA
www.carsondellosa.com

ISBN 978-1-60996-479-5
01-335111151

The **Step-by-Step Problem Solving** series focuses on the underlying processes and strategies essential to problem solving. Each book introduces various skill sets and builds upon them as the level increases. The six-book series covers the following thinking skills and heuristics:

Thinking Skills
- ❑ Analyzing Parts and Wholes
- ❑ Comparing
- ❑ Classifying
- ❑ Identifying Patterns and Relationships
- ❑ Deduction
- ❑ Induction
- ❑ Spatial Visualization

Heuristics
- ❑ Act It Out
- ❑ Draw a Diagram/Model
- ❑ Look for a Pattern
- ❑ Work Backward
- ❑ Make a List/Table
- ❑ Guess and Check
- ❑ Before and After
- ❑ Make Suppositions
- ❑ Use Equations

Students who are keen to develop their problem-solving abilities will learn quickly how to:
- ❑ make sense of the problem: what am I asked to find?
- ❑ make use of given information: what do I know?
- ❑ think of possible strategies: have I come across similar problems before?
- ❑ choose the correct strategy: apply what I know confidently.
- ❑ solve the problem: work out the steps.
- ❑ check the answer: is the solution logical and reasonable?

Practice questions follow each skill-set example, and three graded mixed practices (easy, intermediate, challenging) are provided for an overall assessment of the skills learned. The worked solutions show the application of the strategies used. Students will find this series invaluable in helping them understand and master problem-solving skills.

Table of Contents

Strategy Summary

The following summary provides examples of the various skill sets taught in Step-by-Step Problem Solving.

Page 6 Skill Set 1-A: Analyzing Parts and Wholes

Analyzing parts and wholes is a basic and useful way of looking at a problem. To analyze parts and wholes is to recognize the parts and understand how they form the whole.

Example: There are 8,000 people at a stadium. There are 1,345 women and 3,492 men at the stadium. The rest are children. How many children are there?

Think

• Sort the data: 8,000 people, 1,345 women, 3,492 men, and unknown number of children.

• Identify the whole and the parts:

whole → 8,000, parts → 1,345, 3,492, unknown number of children.

• Draw the part-whole model.

• Find the answer.

Solve

1,345	3,492	?
part (women)	part (men)	part (children)

(whole) 8,000

$1,345 + 3,492 = 4,837$
$8,000 - 4,837 = 3,163$

Answer There are **3,163 children**.

Page 9 Skill Set 1-B: Analyzing Parts and Wholes

Some problems give the parts but not the whole. Use the part-whole model to answer the problems.

Example: A grocery store sells 1,246 cereal bars, 622 energy bars, and 932 granola bars. How many snack bars does the grocery store sell altogether?

Think

• Identify the parts and the whole: parts → 1,246 cereal, 622 energy, and 932 granola;

whole → total number of snack bars.

• Draw the part-whole model.

• Find the answer.

Solve

1,246	622	932
cereal	energy	granola

?

$1,246 + 622 + 932 = 2,800$

Answer The grocery store sells **2,800 snack bars** altogether.

Page 11 Skill Set 2-A: Comparing

Comparing is an effective way of identifying the relationship between the variables in a problem. Comparing the information in a problem helps you determine the differences in variables' quantities (for example, more or less).

Example: Trey has $248. Evan has $345 more than Trey. Nikki has $145 less than Evan. How much money do they have altogether?

Think

• Compare Trey's amount and Evan's amount. Evan has $345 more. Draw a model.

• Compare Evan's amount and Nikki's amount. Nikki has $145 less. Add this data to the model.

• Find the answer.

Solve

Trey: $248
Evan: $248 ... $345
Nikki: $145

Evan → $248 + $345 = $593
Nikki → $593 − $145 = $448
$248 + $593 + $448 = $1,289

Answer They have **$1,289** altogether.

Strategy Summary

Page 14 Skill Set 2-B: Comparing

Some problems give the whole and some of the parts. Use the part-whole model to answer the problems.

Example: There are 2,000 pet owners at a pet convention. There are 630 cat owners and 250 more dog owners than cat owners. If the rest are rabbit owners, how many more dog owners than rabbit owners are there?

Think

- Compare the number of cat owners and the number of dog owners. There are 250 more dog owners. Draw a model.
- There are 2,000 pet owners in total. Add this data to the model.
- Find the answer.

Solve

dog owners → 630 + 250 = 880
rabbit owners → 2,000 − 630 − 880 = 490
880 − 490 = 390

Answer There are **390 more dog owners** than rabbit owners.

Page 16 Skill Set 3-A: Identifying Patterns and Relationships

In number and pattern sequences, a relationship often exists among the data in the given arrangement. Always check the number or pattern sequence using the four operations, +, −, ×, or ÷, or rotate the patterns to find the relationship among the data.

Example: Find the missing numbers in the number pattern.

Think

- Observe the numbers and look for a pattern.
- Try to find the common relationship between the numbers using the four operations (+, −, ×, ÷).
- Identify the pattern and the relationship. Find the answers.

Solve

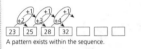

Therefore,

A pattern exists within the sequence.

Answer The missing numbers are **37, 43,** and **50**.

Page 19 Skill Set 3-B: Identifying Patterns and Relationships

Sometimes, creating a table can help you identify the relationship and solve the pattern.

Example: Study the figure. How many triangles are on layer 5?

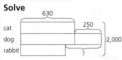

Think

- Count the triangles on each layer and write the data in a table.
- Try to find the common relationship between the numbers using the four operations (+, −, ×, ÷).
- Identify the pattern and the relationship. Find the answer.

Solve

layer	1	2	3	4	5
triangles	2	6	10	14	**18**

Answer There are **18 triangles** on layer 5.

Page 21 Skill Set 4-A: Work Backward

Working backward is a strategy that uses a problem's answer to find the numbers the problem begins with. Very often, you can trace back the steps and reverse the operations to find the answers.

Example: Zane had some treats. He kept 15 treats and gave the rest to 6 friends. Each friend received 8 treats. How many treats did Zane have at first?

Think

- Data: Zane → 15 treats; each friend → 8 treats; 6 friends
- Work backward with the information: 6 friends each received 8 treats.
- Reverse the operations to find the answer.

Solve

Total number of treats given to 6 friends → 8 × 6 = 48
48 + 15 = 63

Answer Zane had **63 treats** at first.

Page 24 Skill Set 4-B: Work Backward

Besides solving word problems, you can also work backward to find a specific number.

Example: *N* is a number. When it is subtracted from 22, and the result is divided by 3, the answer is 5. What number is *N*?

Think

- Data: $22 - N = $ result → result $\div 3 = $ answer $= 5$
- Reverse the operations to find the answer.

Solve

$5 \times 3 = 15$
$22 - 15 = 7$

Answer *N* is **7**.

Page 26 Skill Set 5-A: Draw a Diagram/Model

Drawing diagrams or models helps you organize the data and identify the relationship among the data found in a problem. This skill set is similar to Analyzing Parts and Wholes, but it involves drawing a different type of model.

Example: Mr. Lewis bought a dining table and 6 identical chairs for $1,200. The table cost $300. What was the cost of 1 chair?

Think

- Data: dining table and 6 chairs = $1,200; dining table = $300
- If 6 chairs are identical, each chair is 1 unit.
- Draw a model and fill in the data.

Solve

6 units or 6 chairs → $1,200 − $300 = $900
1 unit or 1 chair → $900 ÷ 6 = $150

Answer The cost of 1 chair was **$150**.

Page 29 Skill Set 5-B: Draw a Diagram/Model

Solving some problems requires drawing a different type of model.

Example: In Mrs. King's class, 3 students like to read comic books. Twice as many students like to read mystery books. Three times that number of students like to read fantasy books more than mystery books. How many students are in the class?

Think

- Data: comic = 3; mystery = 2 × comic; fantasy = 3 × mystery
- Use 1 unit to represent 3 students.
- Draw a model and fill in the data.

Solve

mystery → 2 × 3 = 6
fantasy → 3 × 6 = 18
3 + 6 + 18 = 27

Answer There are **27 students** in the class.

Page 31 Skill Set 6: Look for a Pattern

To look for a pattern among a problem's data, examine the variables to find the specific pattern.

Example: Find the values of X and Y.

Think

- Study the numbers.
- Find the relationships between the numbers within each set to find a repeated pattern in the 3 sets.
- Find the values of X and Y.

Solve

1st set → 3 × 2 = 6
6 + 2 = 8

2nd set → 4 × 2 = 8
8 + 2 = 10
(checked and confirmed)

3rd set → 14 − 2 = 12
(work backward)
12 ÷ 2 = 6
check → **6** × 2 = **12**
12 + 2 = **14**

Answer The value of X is **6**, and the value of Y is **12**.

Page 35 Skill Set 7: Make a List/Table

Making a list or a table of the information given in a problem helps organize the data. This makes it easier to see missing data or recognize patterns.

Example: Store A sells hats for adults and caps for children. Both the hats and the caps come in 3 different sizes: small, medium, and large. If 1 of each type and size of hat and cap were sold last week, how many hats and caps were sold altogether?

Think

- List the different choices: hats and their sizes and caps and their sizes.
- Arrange the choices and count the number of choices in the list.

Solve

item \ size	small	medium	large
hat	✓	✓	✓
cap	✓	✓	✓

Answer There were **6 hats and caps** sold altogether.

Skill Set 1-A: Analyzing Parts and Wholes

Analyzing parts and wholes is a basic and useful way of looking at a problem. To analyze parts and wholes is to recognize the parts and understand how they form the whole.

Example:
There are 8,000 people at a stadium. There are 1,345 women and 3,492 men at the stadium. The rest are children. How many children are there?

 Think
- Sort the data: 8,000 people, 1,345 women, 3,492 men, and unknown number of children.
- Identify the whole and the parts:
  whole → 8,000, parts → 1,345, 3,492, unknown number of children.
- Draw the part-whole model.
- Find the answer.

 Solve

1,345	3,492	?
part (women)	part (men)	part (children)

(whole) 8,000

$1,345 + 3,492 = 4,837$
$8,000 - 4,837 = 3,163$

 Answer There are **3,163 children**.

Give it a try!

A factory produces 7,500 cartons of milk every day. They produce 1,250 cartons of white milk and 2,750 cartons of strawberry milk. The remaining cartons are chocolate flavored. How many cartons of chocolate milk do they produce?

 Think
Fill in the data and find the answer.

 Solve

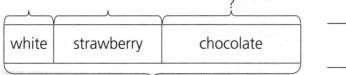

white	strawberry	chocolate

_____ + _____ = _____

_____ − _____ = _____

 Answer They produce _____ **cartons** of chocolate milk.

Practice: Analyzing Parts and Wholes

1. Kelly has 9,000 stamps. She has 6,483 American stamps and 1,248 Asian stamps. The rest of them are European stamps. How many European stamps does Kelly have?

💡 **Think**

✏️ **Solve**

⭐ **Answer**

2. Sean, Riley, and Adam shared $7,500. Sean received $3,242, and Riley received $2,147. How much money did Adam receive?

💡 **Think**

✏️ **Solve**

⭐ **Answer**

Practice: Analyzing Parts and Wholes

3. A shop has 10,000 balloons. There are 3,411 blue balloons and 2,622 red balloons. The rest are yellow. How many yellow balloons are at the shop?

💡 **Think**

✏️ **Solve**

⭐ **Answer**

Skill Set 1-B: Analyzing Parts and Wholes

Some problems give the parts but not the whole. Use the part-whole model to answer the problems.

Example:
A grocery store sells 1,246 cereal bars, 622 energy bars, and 932 granola bars. How many snack bars does the grocery store sell altogether?

 Think

- Identify the parts and the whole: parts → 1,246 cereal, 622 energy, and 932 granola; whole → total number of snack bars.
- Draw the part-whole model.
- Find the answer.

 Solve

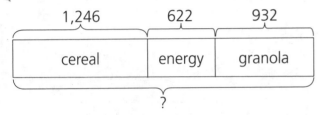

1,246 + 622 + 932 = 2,800

⭐ **Answer** The grocery store sells **2,800 snack bars** altogether.

Give it a try!

A writer types 1,583 words of his new book on Monday. He types 1,247 words on Tuesday and 1,396 words on Wednesday. How many words does the writer type in the 3 days?

 Think
Fill in the data and find the answer.

 Solve

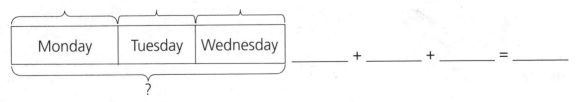

_____ + _____ + _____ = _____

⭐ **Answer** The writer types _____ **words** in the 3 days.

4. Penny, Sally, and Carla went on a trip together. Penny spent $1,244, Sally spent $2,131, and Carla spent $1,345. How much money did they spend altogether?

💡 **Think**

✏️ **Solve**

⭐ **Answer**

5. Daniel bought a computer, a watch, and a sound system. The watch cost $1,249. The computer cost as much as the watch, and the sound system cost $799. How much did he spend altogether?

💡 **Think**

✏️ **Solve**

⭐ **Answer**

Skill Set 2-A: Comparing

Comparing is an effective way of identifying the relationship between the variables in a problem. Comparing the information in a problem helps you determine the differences in variables' quantities (for example, more or less).

Example:

Trey has $248. Evan has $345 more than Trey. Nikki has $145 less than Evan. How much money do they have altogether?

 Think

- Compare Trey's amount and Evan's amount. Evan has $345 more. Draw a model.
- Compare Evan's amount and Nikki's amount. Nikki has $145 less. Add this data to the model.
- Find the answer.

 Solve

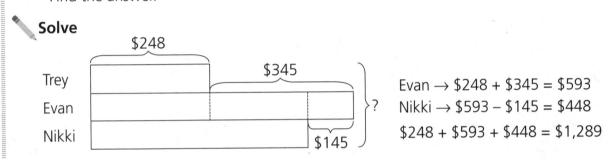

Evan → $248 + $345 = $593
Nikki → $593 − $145 = $448
$248 + $593 + $448 = $1,289

⭐ **Answer** They have **$1,289** altogether.

Give it a try!

There are 372 daisies in a field. There are 206 more roses than daisies and 122 fewer tulips than roses. How many flowers are in the field altogether?

 Think

Fill in the data and find the answer.

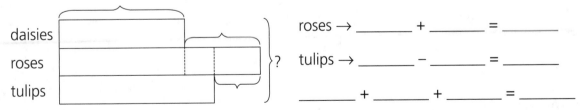 **Solve**

roses → _____ + _____ = _____
tulips → _____ − _____ = _____
_____ + _____ + _____ = _____

⭐ **Answer** There are _____ **flowers** in the field altogether.

(Answer: 1,406)

Practice: Comparing

1. Gavin has 715 marbles. Seth has 48 fewer marbles than Gavin. Gavin has 85 more marbles than Ben. How many marbles do they have altogether?

💡 **Think**

✏️ **Solve**

⭐ **Answer**

2. Kate has 546 stamps. Her sister has 46 fewer stamps than Kate, and her brother has 80 more stamps than Kate. How many stamps do they have altogether?

💡 **Think**

✏️ **Solve**

⭐ **Answer**

3. Peter has 68 craft sticks. Tony has 268 more craft sticks than Peter. Peter has 124 fewer craft sticks than Sam. How many craft sticks do they have altogether?

 Think

 Solve

⭐ **Answer**

Some problems give the whole and some of the parts. Use the part-whole model to answer the problems.

Example:

There are 2,000 pet owners at a pet convention. There are 630 cat owners and 250 more dog owners than cat owners. If the rest are rabbit owners, how many more dog owners than rabbit owners are there?

 Think

- Compare the number of cat owners and the number of dog owners. There are 250 more dog owners. Draw a model.
- There are 2,000 pet owners in total. Add this data to the model.
- Find the answer.

 Solve

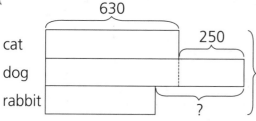

dog owners → 630 + 250 = 880
rabbit owners → 2,000 − 630 − 880 = 490
880 − 490 = 390

⭐ **Answer** There are **390 more dog owners** than rabbit owners.

Give it a try!

Mr. Rivera spent $1,300 while shopping. He spent $398 on a pair of shoes and $352 more on a suit than on the shoes. He spent the remaining money on 2 shirts. If the shirts cost the same, how much did Mr. Rivera spend on each shirt?

 Think

Fill in the data and find the answer.

 Solve

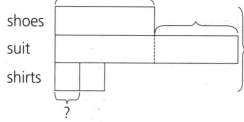

suit →

_____ + _____ = _____

2 shirts →

_____ − _____ − _____ = _____

1 shirt →

_____ ÷ _____ = _____

⭐ **Answer** Mr. Rivera spent _____ on each shirt.

(Answer: $76)

Practice: Comparing

4. There are 6,099 people in a triathlon. There are 2,269 adults and 948 more boys than adults. The rest are girls. How many more adults than girls are there?

💡 **Think**

✏️ **Solve**

⭐ **Answer**

5. There are 1,500 bills in a safe. Of those bills, 495 are $100 bills. There are 86 more $10 bills than $100 bills. The rest are $2 bills. How many $2 bills are in the safe?

💡 **Think**

✏️ **Solve**

⭐ **Answer**

Skill Set 3-A: Identifying Patterns and Relationships

In number and pattern sequences, a relationship often exists among the data in the given arrangement. Always check the number or pattern sequence using the four operations, +, −, ×, or ÷, or rotate the patterns to find the relationship among the data.

Example:
Find the missing numbers in the number pattern.

| 23 | 25 | 28 | 32 | | | |

 Think
- Observe the numbers and look for a pattern.
- Try to find the common relationship between the numbers using the four operations (+, −, ×, ÷).
- Identify the pattern and the relationship. Find the answers.

 Solve

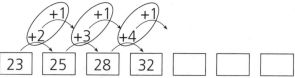

Therefore,

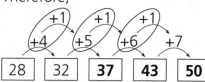

A pattern exists within the sequence.

⭐ **Answer** The missing numbers are **37**, **43**, and **50**.

Give it a try!

Find the missing numbers in the number pattern.

| 41 | 43 | 47 | 53 | | | |

 Think
Identify the pattern and the relationship. Find the answers.

 Solve

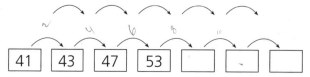

⭐ **Answer** The missing numbers are _____, _____, and _____.

Practice: Identifying Patterns and Relationships

1. Find the missing numbers in the number pattern.

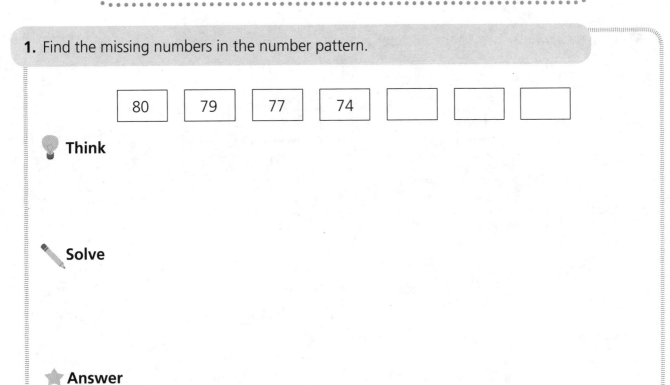

| 80 | 79 | 77 | 74 | | | |

💡 **Think**

✏️ **Solve**

⭐ **Answer**

2. Find the missing numbers in the number pattern.

38   39   37   38

💡 **Think**

✏️ **Solve**

⭐ **Answer**

3. Find the missing numbers in the number pattern.

18	28	38	48	
54	53	52	51	

💡 **Think**

✏️ **Solve**

⭐ **Answer**

Skill Set 3-B: Identifying Patterns and Relationships

Sometimes, creating a table can help you identify the relationship and solve the pattern.

Example:

Study the figure. How many triangles are on layer 5?

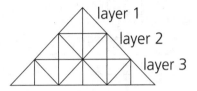

💡 **Think**

- Count the triangles on each layer and write the data in a table.
- Try to find the common relationship between the numbers using the four operations (+, −, ×, ÷).
- Identify the pattern and the relationship. Find the answer.

✏️ **Solve**

layer	1	2	3	4	5
triangles	2	6	10	14	**18**

+ 4   + 4   + 4   + 4

⭐ **Answer** There are **18 triangles** on layer 5.

Give it a try!

A bus is carrying 20 passengers. After a few leave at bus stop 1, there are 17 passengers left. After a few more leave at bus stop 2, there are 14 passengers left. How many passengers are left after bus stop 6?

💡 **Think**

Identify the pattern and the relationship. Find the answer.

✏️ **Solve**

bus stop	0	1	2	3	4	5	6
passengers	20	17	14				

⭐ **Answer** There are _____ **passengers** left after bus stop 6.

(Answer: 2)

Practice: Identifying Patterns and Relationships

4. Some bricks are stacked in the following manner: 1 brick on layer 1, 3 bricks on layer 2, 5 bricks on layer 3, 7 bricks on layer 4, and so on. How many bricks are on layer 8?

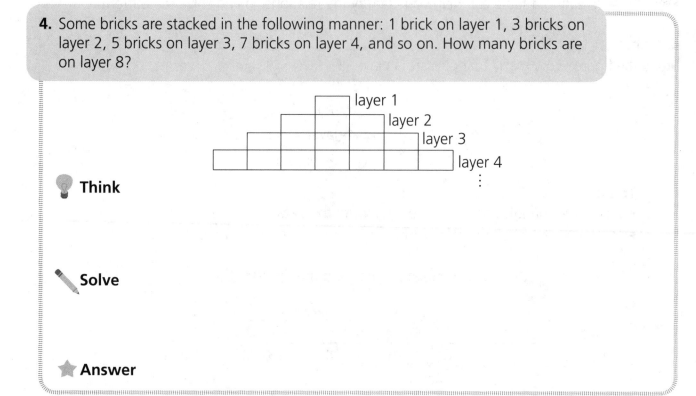

🔆 **Think**

✏️ **Solve**

⭐ **Answer**

5. In a ball game, Shannon would score 2 points for the first catch, 4 points for the second catch, 8 points for the third catch, 16 points for the fourth catch, and so on. How many points would she score for the sixth catch?

🔆 **Think**

✏️ **Solve**

⭐ **Answer**

Working backward is a strategy that uses a problem's answer to find the numbers the problem begins with. Very often, you can trace back the steps and reverse the operations to find the answers.

Example:

Zane had some treats. He kept 15 treats and gave the rest to 6 friends. Each friend received 8 treats. How many treats did Zane have at first?

 Think

- Data: Zane → 15 treats; each friend → 8 treats; 6 friends
- Work backward with the information: 6 friends each received 8 treats.
- Reverse the operations to find the answer.

 Solve

Total number of treats given to 6 friends → 8 × 6 = 48

48 + 15 = 63

 Answer Zane had **63 treats** at first.

Give it a try!

Sarah had some hair clips. She gave 12 hair clips to her sister and the rest to her 3 cousins. Each cousin received 11 hair clips. How many hair clips did Sarah have at first?

 Think

Reverse the operations to find the answer.

 Solve

Total number of hair clips given to 3 cousins

→ _____ × _____ = _____

_____ + _____ = _____

 Answer Sarah had _____ **hair clips** at first.

(Answer: 45)

Practice: Work Backward

1. Garrick has 66 more stickers than Amy. Amy has 44 fewer stickers than Roberto. Roberto has 88 stickers. How many stickers does Garrick have?

💡 **Think**

✏️ **Solve**

⭐ **Answer**

2. Mrs. Fields gave Wendy and her 3 friends 9 muffins each. She has 24 muffins left. How many muffins did Mrs. Fields have at first?

💡 **Think**

✏️ **Solve**

⭐ **Answer**

3. Noah is 6 years older than Darren. Darren is 4 years older than Olivia. Olivia is 12 years old. How old is Noah?

 Think

 Solve

 Answer

Besides solving word problems, you can also work backward to find a specific number.

Example:

N is a number. When it is subtracted from 22, and the result is divided by 3, the answer is 5. What number is *N*?

 Think
- Data: $22 - N = $ result $\rightarrow$ result $\div 3 = $ answer $= 5$
- Reverse the operations to find the answer.

 Solve

$$5 \times 3 = 15$$

$$22 - 15 = 7$$

 Answer *N* is **7**.

Give it a try!

C is a number. When it is multiplied by 4, and 9 is subtracted from the result, the answer is 23. What number is *C*?

 Think
Reverse the operations to find the answer.

 Solve

_____ + _____ = _____

_____ ÷ _____ = _____

 Answer *C* is _____.

(Answer: 8)

4. *A* is a number. When it is added to 4, and the result is multiplied by 6, the answer is 48. What number is *A*?

💡 **Think**

✏️ **Solve**

⭐ **Answer**

5. *B* is a number. When it is subtracted from 100, and the result is divided by 5, the answer is 12. What number is *B*?

💡 **Think**

✏️ **Solve**

⭐ **Answer**

Skill Set 5-A: Draw a Diagram/Model

Drawing diagrams or models helps you organize the data and identify the relationship among the data found in a problem. This skill set is similar to Analyzing Parts and Wholes, but it involves drawing a different type of model.

Example:

Mr. Lewis bought a dining table and 6 identical chairs for $1,200. The table cost $300. What was the cost of 1 chair?

 Think

- Data: dining table and 6 chairs = $1,200; dining table = $300
- If 6 chairs are identical, each chair is 1 unit.
- Draw a model and fill in the data.

 Solve

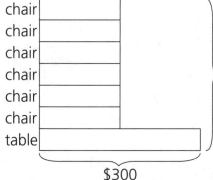

6 units or 6 chairs → $1,200 − $300 = $900

1 unit or 1 chair → $900 ÷ 6 = $150

⭐ **Answer** The cost of 1 chair was **$150**.

Give it a try!

A baker packed 180 cereal bars into 1 big box and 5 small boxes. If the big box contained 60 cereal bars, how many cereal bars did each small box contain?

 Think

Draw a model and fill in the data.

 Solve

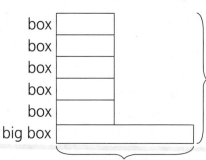

_____ units → _____ − _____ = _____

1 unit → _____ ÷ _____ = _____

⭐ **Answer** Each small box contained _____ **cereal bars**.

(Answer: 24)

1. Dad bought 1 tie and 4 shirts during a sale. He spent a total of $84. The tie cost $20. If the price of each shirt was the same, how much did he pay for each shirt?

💡 **Think**

✏️ **Solve**

⭐ **Answer**

2. A carpenter has 1 board and 5 identical ropes that measure 565 inches. If the board is 165 inches long, how long is each rope?

💡 **Think**

✏️ **Solve**

⭐ **Answer**

3. The total weight of a basket of 9 melons is 19 kilograms 250 grams. If the basket weighs 1 kilogram 250 grams, and each melon has the same weight, how much does each melon weigh?

💡 **Think**

✏️ **Solve**

⭐ **Answer**

Skill Set 5-B: Draw a Diagram/Model

Solving some problems requires drawing a different type of model.

Example:

In Mrs. King's class, 3 students like to read comic books. Twice as many students like to read mystery books. Three times that number of students like to read fantasy books more than mystery books. How many students are in the class?

 Think

- Data: comic = 3; mystery = 2 × comic; fantasy = 3 × mystery
- Use 1 unit to represent 3 students.
- Draw a model and fill in the data.

 Solve

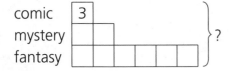

mystery → 2 × 3 = 6
fantasy → 3 × 6 = 18
3 + 6 + 18 = 27

 Answer There are **27 students** in the class.

Give it a try!

At a garage sale, Zoe spent $60 on 1 hat and 2 pairs of shoes. If she spent $9 more on each pair of shoes than on the hat, how much did Zoe spend on the shoes?

 Think

Draw a model and fill in the data.

Solve

_____ units → _____ – _____ – _____

= _____

1 unit → _____ ÷ _____ = _____

_____ units → _____ × _____ = _____

_____ + _____ + _____ = _____

 Answer Zoe spent _____ on the shoes.

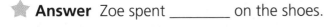

(Answer: $46)

4. Kenan has six times as many stamps as Jose. Jose has twice as many stamps as Drew. Drew has 4 stamps. How many stamps do Kenan and Jose have altogether?

💡 **Think**

✏️ **Solve**

⭐ **Answer**

5. Mr. Upton gave his 3 sons $200 to share among themselves. The oldest son received $20 more than each of the younger sons. How much money did the two younger sons receive altogether?

💡 **Think**

✏️ **Solve**

⭐ **Answer**

Skill Set 6: Look for a Pattern

To look for a pattern among a problem's data, examine the variables to find the specific pattern.

Example:
Find the values of X and Y.

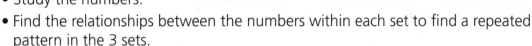

 Think
- Study the numbers.
- Find the relationships between the numbers within each set to find a repeated pattern in the 3 sets.
- Find the values of X and Y.

Solve

1st set → 3 × 2 = 6
  6 + 2 = 8

2nd set → 4 × 2 = 8
  8 + 2 = 10
  (checked and confirmed)

3rd set → 14 − 2 = 12
  (work backward)
  12 ÷ 2 = 6

check → **6** × 2 = **12**
  12 + 2 = 14

⭐ **Answer** The value of X is **6**, and the value of Y is **12**.

Give it a try!

Find the values of A and B.

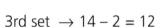

 Think
Find the relationships between the numbers and find the values of A and B.

 Solve

1st set → _____

2nd set → _____

_____
(checked and confirmed)

3rd set → _____

_____
(work backward)

check → _____

_____

⭐ **Answer** The value of A is _____, and the value of B is _____.

Practice: Look for a Pattern

1. Find the values of A and B.

1	2
4	3

2	4
8	6

A	8
16	**B**

8	16
32	24

 Think

 Solve

⭐ **Answer**

2. Study the pattern. Find the missing numbers.

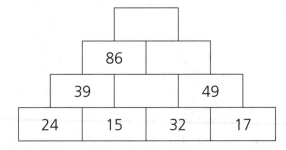

💡 **Think**

✏️ **Solve**

⭐ **Answer**

3. Lily has a torn piece of paper with some numbers on it. Find the values of A, B, and C.

 Think

1	2	3	4	5
2	4	6	8	10
3	6	9	12	15
4	8	12	16	A
5	10	15	B	C

 Solve

 Answer

4. Find the values of X and Y.

 Think

1	2	4	5
X	8	7	6
12	10	Y	11

Solve

Answer

5. Study the sequence of letters. What letter is in the 19th position?

A B C D E E D C B A A B C D E ...
First   15th

 Think

Solve

⭐ **Answer**

Skill Set 7: Make a List/Table

Making a list or a table of the information given in a problem helps organize the data. This makes it easier to see missing data or recognize patterns.

Example:

Store A sells hats for adults and caps for children. Both the hats and the caps come in 3 different sizes: small, medium, and large. If 1 of each type and size of hat and cap were sold last week, how many hats and caps were sold altogether?

 Think

- List the different choices: hats and their sizes and caps and their sizes.
- Arrange the choices and count the number of choices in the list.

 Solve

item size	small	medium	large
hat	✓	✓	✓
cap	✓	✓	✓

 Answer There were **6 hats and caps** sold altogether.

Give it a try!

Pedro has 3 different pens: 1 blue, 1 red, and 1 green. Pedro can mix and match their caps to create different combinations. How many different combinations can Pedro create altogether?

 Think

Make a list of all of the possible combinations and count them.

 Solve

B   B   B

B   R   G _____ _____

 Answer I can create _____ **different combinations** altogether.

(Answer: 9)

Practice: Make a List/Table

1. How many different 3-digit numbers can be formed from the numbers 1, 2, and 3 if the digits do not repeat in the numbers?

💡 **Think**

✏️ **Solve**

⭐ **Answer**

2. Ivan has a 5-cent stamp, a 10-cent stamp, and a 20-cent stamp. How many different combinations of postage can he form with the stamps?

💡 **Think**

✏️ **Solve**

⭐ **Answer**

3. There are 3 empty seats in a classroom: 1 in the first row, 1 in the second row, and 1 in the third row. Rachel and Mario are new students. How many ways can the teacher seat them?

💡 **Think**

✏️ **Solve**

⭐ **Answer**

4. Mrs. Ortiz needs 2 students: 1 to be the class monitor and 1 to be the assistant monitor. She has 2 boys, Leo and Scott, and 2 girls, Laura and Sandra, volunteer for the positions. How many ways can Mrs. Ortiz pair them if she wants a boy and a girl for the positions?

💡 **Think**

✏️ **Solve**

⭐ **Answer**

5. Travis owns a frozen yogurt shop. He offers 3 flavors of yogurt: strawberry, mango, and peach. The yogurt can be served in cups, bowls, and cones. How many different combinations can he offer his customers if they can choose 1 flavor of yogurt served in a cup, a bowl, or a cone?

 Think

 Solve

⭐ **Answer**

Mixed Practice: Easy

1. The total age of Dad, Mom, and Patrick is 203 years old. Dad is 87 years old, and Mom is 76 years old. How old is Patrick?

💡 **Think**

✏️ **Solve**

⭐ **Answer**

2. Cathy spent $88 on a dress and $62 on a blouse. She had $145 left. How much money did she have at first?

💡 **Think**

✏️ **Solve**

⭐ **Answer**

3. There are 16 books on each of 5 shelves on a wall and 15 books on the sixth shelf. How many books are on the shelves altogether?

💡 **Think**

✏️ **Solve**

⭐ **Answer**

4. There were 60 children and 8 tables. An equal number of children sat at each table, and 12 children were left without seats. How many children were seated at each table?

💡 **Think**

✏️ **Solve**

⭐ **Answer**

5. Find the missing numbers in the number pattern.

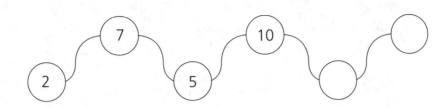

 Think

 Solve

 Answer

6. Libby has $15 more than Fiona. Kit has $10 more than Libby. Fiona has $48. How much money does Kit have?

💡 **Think**

✏️ **Solve**

 Answer

7. Find the value of A.

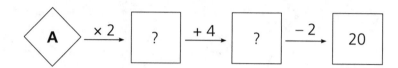

A   ×2 → ?   +4 → ?   −2 → 20

 Think

 Solve

 Answer

8. A pen costs \$2 and a writing pad costs \$3. Jay wants to buy an equal number of pens and writing pads for his friends. How much will he have to spend on writing pads if he spends \$12 on pens?

 Think

 Solve

Answer

9. How many squares are in the figure?

💡 **Think**

✏️ **Solve**

⭐ **Answer**

---

10. Find the missing numbers in the number pattern.

1,   3,   4,   7,   11,   (   ), (   )

💡 **Think**

✏️ **Solve**

⭐ **Answer**

Mixed Practice: Easy

11. At an education fair, 6,593 students signed up for classes. Some 1,445 students signed up for art classes, 2,736 signed up for language classes, and the rest signed up for computer classes. How many students signed up for computer classes?

💡 **Think**

✏️ **Solve**

⭐ **Answer**

12. Mrs. Robertson used 1,000 grams of flour to make some pastries. She used 220 grams to make a pie and 180 grams more than that to make a cake. If she used the rest to make 4 muffins, how much flour did Mrs. Robertson use to make each muffin?

💡 **Think**

✏️ **Solve**

⭐ **Answer**

Mixed Practice: Intermediate

1. In 1 week, Janelle earns $268. Reese earns $125 more than Janelle. How much money do they earn in 4 weeks?

💡 **Think**

✏️ **Solve**

⭐ **Answer**

2. Lindsey has a total of 4,500 black, blue, and red pens. She has 2,512 black pens. She has 678 fewer blue pens than black pens. The rest are red pens. How many red pens does Lindsey have?

💡 **Think**

✏️ **Solve**

⭐ **Answer**

3. Mrs. Beck paid a total of $34 for 4 identical bowls and 2 identical plates. A bowl cost $4 more than a plate. How much did she pay for each bowl?

💡 **Think**

✏️ **Solve**

⭐ **Answer**

4. A dictionary costs $24. The total cost of the dictionary and 4 identical diaries is the same as 7 diaries. How much does 1 diary cost?

💡 **Think**

✏️ **Solve**

⭐ **Answer**

5. A farmer had 2,000 eggs. He sold 450 of them and packed the remaining eggs into cartons of 6 each. How many eggs were not packed into the cartons?

 Think

 Solve

⭐ **Answer**

6. Study the numbers in the number grid. What is the fourth number in the 10th row?

 Think

1st row	1	2	3	4	5
2nd row	6	7	8	9	10
3rd row	11	12	13	14	15
⋮					
10th row				?	

 Solve

⭐ **Answer**

7. Denise baked 4 loaves of bread on Monday, 6 loaves on Tuesday, 8 loaves on Wednesday, and so on. If she increased the number of loaves she baked every day at the same rate, how many loaves of bread did she bake during the week?

💡 **Think**

✏️ **Solve**

⭐ **Answer**

8. At a tournament, 28 chess matches were played. If each player was allowed to play only once with every other player, how many players were there altogether?

💡 **Think**

✏️ **Solve**

⭐ **Answer**

9. Sabena had a sum of money. She spent $10 on a textbook and used half of the remaining money to buy some fruit. She then bought a meal that cost $5 and was left with $8. How much money did Sabena have at first?

💡 **Think**

✏️ **Solve**

⭐ **Answer**

10. How many handshakes would be exchanged if 10 people all shook hands with each other once?

💡 **Think**

✏️ **Solve**

⭐ **Answer**

11. Find the missing numbers in the number pattern.

| 50 | 47 | 49 | 46 | | | |

💡 **Think**

✏️ **Solve**

⭐ **Answer**

12. *X* is a number. It is divided by 3, and 5 is subtracted from the result. The new result is then multiplied by 7. If the final answer is 28, what number is *X*?

💡 **Think**

✏️ **Solve**

⭐ **Answer**

Mixed Practice: Challenging

1. Holly left her apartment and walked up 3 floors to return a book to Kayla. She then went down 4 floors to Paige's place to get the class notes from her. Finally, Holly walked up 2 floors to look for Jenna, who was not home. If Jenna lives on the eighth floor, which floor does Holly live on?

 Think

 Solve

⭐ **Answer**

2. Study the pattern. What numbers are in set 19?

Set 1			Set 2			Set 3			⋯	Set 19		
1	2	6	2	4	12	3	6	18				

 Think

 Solve

⭐ **Answer**

3. Alicia, Bill, and Ross are in Group A. David, Maddie, and Shelby are in Group B. The students are going to have their pictures taken. They will stand in 2 rows by group, and group members cannot be separated. If 2 girls or 2 boys cannot be standing next to each other, how many different ways can they be arranged in a row?

💡 **Think**

✏️ **Solve**

⭐ **Answer**

4. Becky has $60 and Nina has $120. How much money must Becky give to Nina so that the amount of money Nina has is 5 times what Becky has?

💡 **Think**

✏️ **Solve**

⭐ **Answer**

5. Study the problems.

$$\star + \star + \star = \Box + \Box$$

$$\star + \star + \star + \Box + \Box = 120$$

What is $\star + \Box$?

💡 **Think**

✏️ **Solve**

⭐ **Answer**

---

6. A toy maker packed 29 boxes with 9 tops each and had 3 tops left. How many more boxes of tops would he have if he had packed 3 tops into each box instead?

💡 **Think**

✏️ **Solve**

⭐ **Answer**

7. There were 480 chairs and 3 times as many stools in a hall. The chairs and the stools were arranged together randomly in rows of 8. How many rows of chairs and stools were there?

💡 **Think**

✏️ **Solve**

⭐ **Answer**

8. Mr. Gupta bought 3 identical watches and had $450 left. If he spent 4 times as much as the amount of money he had left, how much did each watch cost?

💡 **Think**

✏️ **Solve**

⭐ **Answer**

9. Mrs. Murphy spent $49.60 on 2 textbooks and 3 workbooks. Each textbook cost $12.50. How much did Mrs. Murphy spend on each workbook if they cost the same?

💡 **Think**

✏️ **Solve**

⭐ **Answer**

10. A mango weighs 36 ounces. The total weight of 3 mangoes and 1 apple is the same as the weight of 5 apples. How much does 1 apple weigh?

💡 **Think**

✏️ **Solve**

⭐ **Answer**

11. Find the values of M and N.

1	2		3	4		M	6		7	8
5	3		11	7		17	11		N	15

 Think

 Solve

 Answer

12. Miguel has 3 different counters: 1 blue, 1 red, and 1 yellow. How many different color combinations can he make with more than 1 counter?

 Think

Solve

Answer

13. Natalie had some marbles. She gave $\frac{1}{3}$ of them to her brother, who kept 12 marbles for himself and gave the rest to 5 friends. If each friend received 7 marbles, how many marbles did Natalie have at first?

 Think

 Solve

⭐ **Answer**

14. Find the missing numbers in the number pattern.

| 20 | 21 | 19 | 22 | | | |

💡 **Think**

✏️ **Solve**

⭐ **Answer**

Answer Key

Analyzing Parts and Wholes
pages 6–10

1.
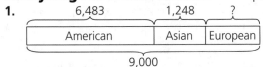

6,483 + 1,248 = 7,731
9,000 − 7,731 = 1,269
She has **1,269 European stamps**.

2.
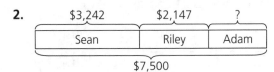

$3,242 + $2,147 = $5,389
$7,500 − $5,389 = $2,111
Adam received **$2,111**.

3.
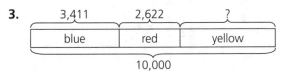

3,411 + 2,622 = 6,033
10,000 − 6,033 = 3,967
There are **3,967 yellow balloons** at the shop.

4.
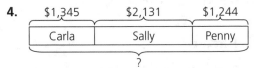

$1,345 + $2,131 + $1,244 = $4,720
They spent **$4,720** altogether.

5.
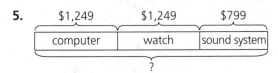

$1,249 + $1,249 = $2,498
$2,498 + $799 = $3,297
He spent **$3,297** altogether.

Comparing
pages 11–15

1.
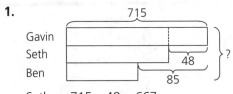

Seth → 715 − 48 = 667
Ben → 715 − 85 = 630
715 + 667 + 630 = 2,012
They have **2,012 marbles** altogether.

2.
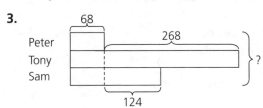

sister → 546 − 46 = 500
brother → 546 + 80 = 626
546 + 500 + 626 = 1,672
They have **1,672 stamps** altogether.

3.
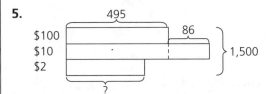

Tony → 68 + 268 = 336
Sam → 68 + 124 = 192
68 + 336 + 192 = 596
They have **596 craft sticks** altogether.

4.
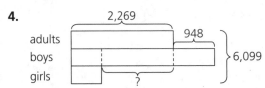

boys → 2,269 + 948 = 3,217
girls → 6,099 − 2,269 − 3,217 = 613
2,269 − 613 = 1,656
There are **1,656 more adults** than girls.

5.
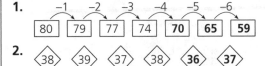

$10 bills → 495 + 86 = 581
$2 bills → 1,500 − 495 − 581 = 424
There are **424 $2 bills** in the safe.

Identifying Patterns and Relationships
pages 16–20

1.
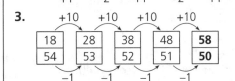

2.

3.

4.

layer	1	2	3	4	5	6	7	8
brick(s)	1	3	5	7	9	11	13	**15**

+2 +2 +2 +2 +2 +2 +2

There are **15 bricks** on layer 8.

5.

catch	1st	2nd	3rd	4th	5th	6th
points	2	4	8	16	32	64

×2 ×2 ×2 ×2 ×2

She would score **64 points** for the 6th catch.

Work Backward pages 21–25

1. Amy → 88 − 44 = 44
Garrick → 44 + 66 = 110
Garrick has **110 stickers**.

2. 1 + 3 = 4
There were 4 children.
9 × 4 = 36
She gave 36 muffins to the children.
36 + 24 = 60
She had **60 muffins** at first.

3. Darren → 12 + 4 = 16
Noah → 16 + 6 = 22
Noah is **22 years old**.

4. 48 ÷ 6 = 8
8 − 4 = 4
A is **4**.

5. 12 × 5 = 60
100 − 60 = 40
B is **40**.

Draw a Diagram/Model pages 26–30

1.

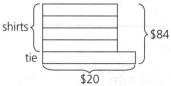

4 shirts → $84 − $20 = $64
1 shirt → $64 ÷ 4 = $16
He paid **$16** for each shirt.

2.

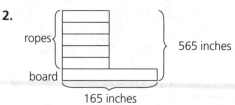

5 ropes → 565 inches − 165 inches = 400 inches

1 rope → 400 inches ÷ 5 = 80 inches
Each rope is **80 inches** long.

3.

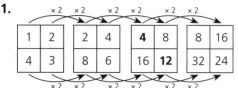

9 melons → 19 kilograms 250 grams − 1 kilogram 250 grams = 18 kilograms

1 melon → 18 kilograms ÷ 9 = 2 kilograms
Each melon weighs **2 kilograms**.

4.

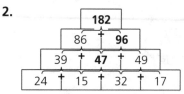

Jose → 4 × 2 = 8
Kenan → 8 × 6 = 48
8 + 48 = 56
They have **56 stamps** altogether.

5.

oldest / younger — 1 unit, 1 unit, 1 unit — $20 — $200

3 units → $200 − $20 = $180
1 unit → $180 ÷ 3 = $60
2 units → $60 × 2 = $120
They received **$120** altogether.

Look for a Pattern pages 31–34

1.

×2 ×2 ×2 ×2 ×2 ×2

1	2		2	4		**4**	8		8	16
4	3		8	6		16	**12**		32	24

×2 ×2 ×2 ×2 ×2 ×2

A = **4**, B = **12**

2.

```
            182
        86  †  96
     39  †  47  †  49
  24  †  15  †  32  †  17
```

3. Multiplication tables 4 or 5:

20
20 25

4.

1	2	4	5
X	8	7	6
12	10	**Y**	11
12 − 1 = **11**	2 + 8 = 10	4 + 7 = **11**	5 + 6 = 11

X = **11**, Y = **11**.

5. A B C D E E D C B A A B C D E [E] [D] [C] [B]
                                       16th   19th
                    ↑
                 pattern repeats

The letter **B** is in the 19th position.

Make a List/Table
pages 35–38

1. Make a list: 1 2 3   1 3 2
                  2 3 1   2 1 3
                  3 2 1   3 1 2
There are **6 different 3-digit numbers** that can be formed.

2. Values formed with 1 stamp: 5¢, 10¢, 20¢
Values formed with 2 stamps: 5¢ + 10¢ = 15¢
                                     5¢ + 20¢ = 25¢
                               10¢ + 20¢ = 30¢
Values formed with 3 stamps: 5¢ + 10¢ + 20¢
                                   = 35¢
He can form **7 different values** of postage.

3.

1st row	2nd row	3rd row
Rachel	Mario	–
Mario	Rachel	–
Mario	–	Rachel
Rachel	–	Mario
–	Mario	Rachel
–	Rachel	Mario

The teacher can seat them in **6 ways**.

4.

monitor	assistant
Leo	Laura
Laura	Leo
Leo	Sandra
Sandra	Leo
Scott	Laura
Laura	Scott
Scott	Sandra
Sandra	Scott

There are **8 ways** to pair them.

5.

	strawberry
cup	mango
	peach
	strawberry
bowl	mango
	peach
	strawberry
cone	mango
	peach

He can offer **9 combinations**.

Mixed Practice: Easy
pages 39–44

1.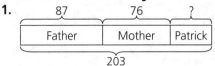

| Father | Mother | Patrick |

203

87 + 76 = 163
203 – 163 = 40
Patrick is **40 years old**.

2.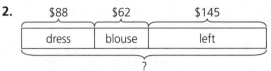

| dress | blouse | left |

?

$88 + $62 + $145 = $295
She had **$295** at first.

3.

| 16 | 16 | 16 | 16 | 16 | 15 |

?

16 × 5 = 80
80 + 15 = 95
There are **95 books** on the shelves altogether.

4.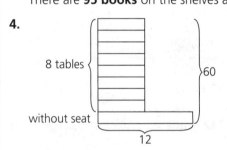

seated → 60 – 12 = 48
48 ÷ 8 = 6
There were **6 children** seated at each table.

5.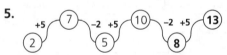

The missing numbers are **8** and **13**.

6.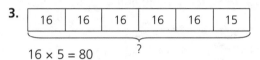

From the model: Kit → $48 + $15 + $10 = $73
Kit has **$73**.

7. Working backward:
20 + 2 = 22
22 – 4 = 18
18 ÷ 2 = 9
A is **9**.

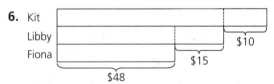

8.

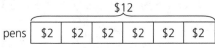

The 6 pens cost $12.
6 writing pads → 6 × $3 = $18
He will have to spend **$18**.

9.

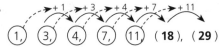

9 squares made up of □

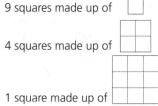

4 squares made up of

1 square made up of

9 + 4 + 1 = 14
There are **14 squares** in the figure.

10.

The missing numbers are **18** and **29**.

11.

1,445	2,736	?
art	language	computer

6,593

1,445 + 2,736 = 4,181
6,593 − 4,181 = 2,412
There are **2,412 students** signed up for computer classes.

12.

cake → 220 grams + 180 grams = 400 grams
4 muffins → 1,000 grams − 220 grams − 400 grams
= 380 grams
1 muffin → 380 ÷ 4 = 95 grams
Mrs. Robertson used **95 grams** of flour to make each muffin.

Mixed Practice: Intermediate   pages 45–50

1.

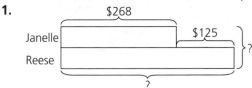

Reese → $268 + $125 = $393
in 1 week → $268 + $393 = $661
in 4 weeks → $661 × 4 = $2,644

They earn **$2,644** in 4 weeks.

2.

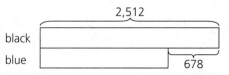

blue → 2,512 − 678 = 1,834
blue + black → 1,834 + 2,512 = 4,346

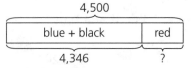

red → 4,500 − 4,346 = 154
She has **154 red pens**.

3.

bowl	1 unit	$4
	1 unit	$4
	1 unit	$4
	1 unit	$4
plate	1 unit	
	1 unit	

$34

$4 × 4 = $16
6 units → $34 − $16 = $18
1 unit → $18 ÷ 6 = $3
$3 + $4 = $7
She paid **$7** for a bowl.

4.

$24

dictionary	d	d	d	d
d	d	d	d	d	d	d

3 diaries = $24
1 diary → $24 ÷ 3 = $8
One diary costs **$8**.

5.

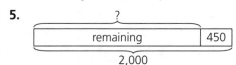

2,000 − 450 = 1,550
1,550 ÷ 6 = 258 r2
There were **2 eggs** not packed into the cartons.

6. The last number of each row is a multiple of 5.
row 1 = 5 → (5 × 1)
row 2 = 10 → (5 × 2)
row 3 = 15 → (5 × 3)
row 10 → 5 × 10 = 50
50 − 1 = 49
The fourth number in the 10th row is **49**.

7.

Mon	Tue	Wed	Thu	Fri	Sat	Sun
4	6	8	10	12	14	16

+2 +2 +2 +2 +2 +2

4 + 6 + 8 + 10 + 12 + 14 + 16 = 70
She baked **70 loaves of bread** during the week.

8. Make a table:
- game played

	A	B	C	D	E	F	G	H	
A		•	•	•	•	•	•	•	7
B			•	•	•	•	•	•	6
C				•	•	•	•	•	5
D					•	•	•	•	4
E						•	•	•	3
F							•	•	2
G								•	1
H									

$7 + 6 + 5 + 4 + 3 + 2 + 1 = 28$

player A to H = 8 players

There were **8 players**.

9. Working backward:

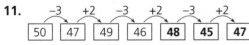

$\$8 + \$5 = \$13$
$\$13 \times 2 = \$26$
$\$26 + \$10 = \$36$

Check: $\$36 \xrightarrow{-\$10} \$26 \xrightarrow{\div 2} \$13 \xrightarrow{-\$5} \$8$

Sabena had **\$36** at first.

10. Make a table:
- handshake

	1	2	3	4	5	6	7	8	9	10	
1		•	•	•	•	•	•	•	•	•	9
2			•	•	•	•	•	•	•	•	8
3				•	•	•	•	•	•	•	7
4					•	•	•	•	•	•	6
5						•	•	•	•	•	5
6							•	•	•	•	4
7								•	•	•	3
8									•	•	2
9										•	1
10											

$9 + 8 + 7 + 6 + 5 + 4 + 3 + 2 + 1 = 45$

There would be **45 handshakes** exchanged.

11.

$$50 \xrightarrow{-3} 47 \xrightarrow{+2} 49 \xrightarrow{-3} 46 \xrightarrow{+2} 48 \xrightarrow{-3} 45 \xrightarrow{+2} 47$$

The missing numbers are **48**, **45**, and **47**.

12. $28 \div 7 = 4$
$4 + 5 = 9$
$9 \times 3 = 27$
X is **27**.

Mixed Practice: Challenging   pages 51–58

1. Working backward:

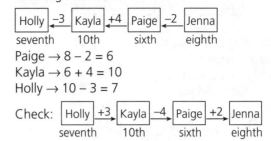

Paige → 8 − 2 = 6
Kayla → 6 + 4 = 10
Holly → 10 − 3 = 7

Check:
| Holly | +3 | Kayla | −4 | Paige | +2 | Jenna |
seventh — 10th — sixth — eighth

Holly lives on the **seventh floor**.

2.

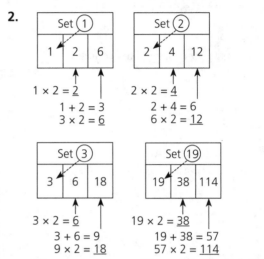

$1 \times 2 = \underline{2}$
$1 + 2 = 3$
$3 \times 2 = \underline{6}$

$2 \times 2 = \underline{4}$
$2 + 4 = 6$
$6 \times 2 = \underline{12}$

$3 \times 2 = \underline{6}$
$3 + 6 = 9$
$9 \times 2 = \underline{18}$

$19 \times 2 = \underline{38}$
$19 + 38 = 57$
$57 \times 2 = \underline{114}$

The numbers in set 19 are **19**, **38**, and **114**.

3. In Group A, Alicia must be in the middle.
In Group B, David must be in the middle.

(1) $\underbrace{B\ A\ R}_{A}\ \underbrace{M\ D\ S}_{B}$ (3) $\underbrace{M\ D\ S}_{B}\ \underbrace{B\ A\ R}_{A}$

(2) $\underbrace{R\ A\ B}_{A}\ \underbrace{S\ D\ M}_{B}$ (4) $\underbrace{S\ D\ M}_{B}\ \underbrace{R\ A\ B}_{A}$

They can be arranged in **4 different ways**.

4. After:

Nina
Becky   } \$120 + \$60

6 units → \$120 + \$60 = \$180
Becky → 1 unit → \$180 ÷ 6 = \$30
\$60 − \$30 = \$30
Becky must give Nina **\$30**.

5.
$$☆ + ☆ + ☆ = □ + □$$
$$\underbrace{☆ + ☆ + ☆}_{□ + □} + □ + □ = 120$$
$4□ = 120$
$□ = 120 \div 4 = 30$
$3☆ = 2 \times 30 = 60$
$☆ = 60 \div 3 = 20$
$☆ + □ = 20 + 30 = 50$
The value of ☆ + □ is **50**.

6.

Working backward:
$29 \times 9 = 261$
$261 + 3 = 264$
There are 264 tops.

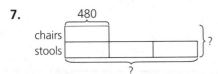

Number of boxes with 3 tops →
$264 \div 3 = 88$
$88 - 29 = 59$
He would have **59 more boxes** of tops.

7.

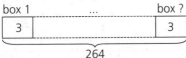

stools → $3 \times 480 = 1,440$
$1,440 + 480 = 1,920$ (chairs and stools)

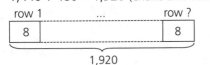

$1,920 \div 8 = 240$
There were **240 rows**.

8.

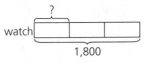

$\$450 \times 4 = \$1,800$

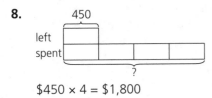

$\$1,800 \div 3 = \$600$
Each watch cost **$600**.

9.

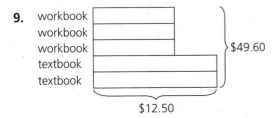

1 unit (textbook) → $12.50
2 units (textbook) → $12.50 × 2 = $25.00
3 units (workbook) → $49.60 − $25.00 = $24.60
1 unit (workbook) → $24.60 ÷ 3 = $8.20
Mrs. Murphy spent **$8.20** on each workbook.

10.

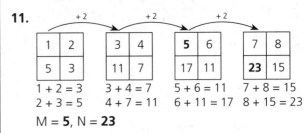

4 apples → 36 oz. × 3 = 108 oz.
1 apple → 108 oz. ÷ 4 = 27 oz.
One apple weighs **27 oz.**

11.

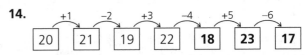

$1 + 2 = 3$ $3 + 4 = 7$ $5 + 6 = 11$ $7 + 8 = 15$
$2 + 3 = 5$ $4 + 7 = 11$ $6 + 11 = 17$ $8 + 15 = 23$

M = **5**, N = **23**

12. with 2 counters → BR, BY, RY, RB, YB, YR (6)
with 3 counters → BRY, BYR, RBY, RYB, YBR, YRB (6)
$6 + 6 = 12$
He can make **12 different color combinations**.

13. $7 \times 5 = 35$
$35 + 12 = 47$
$47 \times 3 = 141$
Natalie had **141 marbles** at first.

14.

| 20 | 21 | 19 | 22 | **18** | **23** | **17** |

+1   −2   +3   −4   +5   −6

The missing numbers are **18**, **23**, and **17**.